M000215674

MARY
the Mother of God

Regina
CLASSICS

Written by Rev. Victor Hoagland, C.P.
Illustrated by Hector Garrido

The Regina Press
New York

This book is dedicated to Charles J. Malhame, our grandfather. His great devotion to the Blessed Mother was responsible for the founding of The Regina Press.

George and Robert

The Regina Press would like to thank Theresa Waller and Laurie Newsham for their invaluable help with this project.

The scripture quotations contained herein are from the New Revised Version Bible: Catholic Edition © 1989 by the Division of Christian Education of the National Council of the Churches of Christ in the U.S.A. Used by permission. All rights reserved.

ISBN: 088271-624-7

Printed in Hong Kong

TABLE OF CONTENTS

INTRODUCTION

Mary, the Mother of God

No woman ever born has attracted more interest than Mary, the Mother of Jesus. True, the four gospels offer few details about her. In the New Testament she is overshadowed by her mighty Son. Yet for almost two thousand years, Christians have cherished her memory.

Why are we drawn to her? Because there was no one closer to Jesus Christ. From his conception and birth, through the greater part of his life, till the days of his death and resurrection, the lives of Son and Mother were bound together. Why would we not wish to know and honor her?

She is a key to the mystery of the Incarnation. Puzzling over the angel's message, wondering at her Child in a manger, raising him in the tiny town of Nazareth, following him to the cross and rejoicing at his resurrection, Mary is a model for those who want to know Jesus Christ. She "treasured all these things and kept them at her heart." From her we learn a pilgrim's faith.

Long ago she was called "Blessed among women." She brings us blessings today. Her story has been told before. Using threads of scripture, history and tradition, the insights of artists and mystics and the feasts of the church, we tell her story again.

Hector Garrido. *Madonna and Child, (Contemporary)*   1

LIFE OF MARY

Mary, the Mother of Jesus

Her name was Mary, a form of the name Miriam, the famous sister of Moses. The name was common among Jewish women in those days.

A well-known tradition says Mary was born in Jerusalem, the daughter of Joachim and Ann. Other early sources say Mary was born in Nazareth. There is even an ancient record that points to Sepphoris, a town a few miles from Nazareth, as her birthplace.

Wherever she was born, Mary's life most likely unfolded in the staunch Jewish settlement of Nazareth in the hills of Galilee, not far from the important caravan routes linking Egypt and Mesopotamia.

The Jewish people were strong and robust. The hill climate was dry and healthful and the land often lacked water. No one knew from one year to the next if enough rain would fall or if invading locusts or field mice would spoil the crops. Facing uncertainty only made the people of Galilee more hardworking and close-knit. Struggling for a living deepened their religious spirit. They

Leonardo Da Vinci. *Saint Anne, Virgin Mary and Child Jesus*, (1452-1519)

learned you must depend always on God.

Her Daily Life

Mary was a woman of rural Galilee and most likely lived in a small family house of stone and mud-brick. She worked like any young girl, grinding wheat and barley into flour, preparing dishes of beans, vegetables, eggs, fruit, nuts and occasional chunks of mutton. Wool had to be made into clothing. Bread had to be baked. A few chickens and a donkey had to be fed. And in the village, small as it was, there were always little children to care for.

Almost daily, she carried a large jar of water from the town well for washing and cooking (the well still supplies modern Nazareth today and is called "Mary's Well"). Early on, the Jewish people found that cleanliness prevented disease, so frequent washing, an important chore of women, became part of their religious practice. The well also was a favorite spot where women talked and traded bits of everyday news.

Just as for the other women of Nazareth, the seasons and times of harvest determined what Mary had to do. With the first downpour of rain in October, the vital wheat crop was sown on the mountain fields, to be gathered, if all went well, in May. Small dark olives, knocked from dull green trees in September, had to be pressed into oil for lamps and food. In May or June, early figs were harvested; in July, the softer juicy fruit. Grapes and pomegranates ripened in September and October. God blessed the hills of Galilee with his bounty, but it could never be taken for granted. The unpredictable land could just as well give nothing to those working it.

From the people of Nazareth, Mary learned about life. Few strangers visited the town. It had little wealth, culture or learning. But just as a tiny drop of water displays a wealth of organisms, the small town of Nazareth had a rich life of its own. Children were born, young people married, others died and were buried. Mary felt these joys and sorrows. A sheep was lost, a family quarreled, a son left home. From such small things, life's deepest lessons could be learned.

Her Rich Faith

The people of Nazareth had a strong Jewish faith. As God's chosen people, descendants of Abraham, Isaac and Jacob, the Jewish people believed this land was theirs, given to their ancestors whom Moses led out of Egypt. They knew by heart the deeds of kings like David and Solomon and the words of prophets like Isaiah and Elijah. Even though the Romans, with Herod's family as their puppets, now occupied Palestine, the Jews of Galilee believed God would someday send a Messiah who would free Israel from her enemies.

They lived in a war-torn land. For centuries before the Roman occupation, conquering armies of Babylonians, Assyrians, Persians and Greeks fought over Palestine. Despite their wars, revolts and riots, the Jews remained a subject people - taxed, bullied and despised by succeeding rulers.

Like their compatriots, the Jews of Nazareth were never far from the dangers of political violence. During the Jewish uprising in Galilee around six A.D., when Jesus was a child, Roman legions captured the city of Sepphoris, five miles from Nazareth; sold all its inhabitants into slavery and burned the city to the ground.

For some Jews, foreign domination only fanned the fires of revolution more brightly in their hearts. Others, like the Pharisees, became

Sassoferrato. *Our Lady of Sorrows,* (1605-1685)

more strictly conservative and exclusive in their religious practices. Still others, like Mary and many ordinary people of the land, became more and more aware that they were powerless themselves, but God, the all-powerful, could raise up the lowly. Their faith was of the deepest kind:

> *Hear, O Israel: The Lord is our God, the Lord alone. You shall love the Lord your God with all your heart, and with all your soul, and with all your might.*
>
> *(Deuteronomy 6:4-5) NRSV*

Mary's faith was strong. Yet, in fervently religious Nazareth with its high moral standards, she hardly stood out at all, even in the eyes of those who knew her best.

When she was fifteen or so, Mary's parents made plans for her to be married, as was customary in those days. They chose Joseph of Nazareth, a carpenter, to be her husband. The engagement took place and Mary returned home to wait about a year before she would go to live with her husband as his wife. But then, something happened:

In the sixth month the angel Gabriel was

Hector Garrido. *The Annunciation* (Contemporary)

sent by God to a town in Galilee called Nazareth, to a virgin engaged to a man whose name was Joseph, of the house of David. The virgin's name was Mary. And he came to her and said, "Greeting, favored one! The Lord is with you." But she was much perplexed by his words and pondered what sort of greeting this might be. The angel said to her, "Do not be afraid, Mary, for you have found favor with God. And now, you will conceive in your womb and bear a son, and you will name him Jesus. He will be great and will be called the Son of the Most High, and the Lord God will give him the throne of his ancestor David. He will reign over the house of Jacob forever, and of his kingdom there will be no end." Mary said to the angel, "How can this be, since I am a virgin?" The angel said to her, "The Holy Spirit will come upon you, and the power of the Most High will overshadow you; therefore the child to be born will be holy; he will be called Son of God. And now, your relative Elizabeth in her old age has also conceived a son; and this is the sixth month for her who was said to be barren. For nothing is impossible with God." Then Mary said, "Here I am, the servant of the Lord; let it be with me according to your

word." Then the angel departed from her.
(Luke 1:26-38) NRSV

The gospels, compiled years after these events at Nazareth, tell the story of Jesus and recall Mary only incidentally. True, St. Luke's account sees Mary favored by God, the Lord's handmaid, a model believer. His story describes her fear and perplexity, her faith and acceptance during the angel's visit. But still, we are left to ourselves to imagine Mary's life and her experience when the angel left her.

The angel's message struck like lightning, changing everything for her. Immense joy filled the young girl's soul when she conceived the child by the power of the Holy Spirit. But when the angel left, Mary was alone.

Living with Mystery

Nazareth certainly was unaware of the angel's visit. That day and the days afterward, men tended the fields, the aroma of fresh bread filled the village air and women talked around the well. The Word of God was made flesh, but the people of Nazareth saw nothing changed. In their eyes Mary was still a young girl of sixteen espoused to Joseph the carpenter.

Once the angel left, Mary faced some troubling questions with only faith to guide her. What about her marriage to Joseph? Since she was bearing a child that was not his, Mary had to face the anguishing prospect of divorce and the shame it could bring down upon her in a small town that frowned on an unfaithful wife. Even though he had a high regard for her, how could she explain to Joseph the mysterious act of God and an angel no one else saw?

The threat was removed when an angel appeared to Joseph in a dream and said: "Joseph, son of David, do not be afraid to take Mary home as your wife, because she has conceived by the Holy Spirit. She will give birth to a son and you must name him Jesus."

When Joseph awakened, he took Mary as his wife to his home. Together they would do what God would have them do.

Mary Visits Her Cousin

Three months after the angel's annunciation, Mary visited her relative Elizabeth, the elderly wife of Zachary who served as a priest in the Temple at Jerusalem. Mary had been told that this couple

Philippe De Champaigne. *The Nativity,* (1602-1674)

advanced in age was to have a child, too, "for nothing is impossible with God."

> *In those days Mary set out and went with haste to a Judean town in the hill country, where she entered the house of Zechariah and greeted Elizabeth. When Elizabeth heard Mary's greeting, the child leaped in her womb. And Elizabeth was filled with the Holy Spirit and exclaimed with a loud cry, "Blessed are you among women, and blessed is the fruit of your womb. And why has this happened to me, that the mother of my Lord comes to me? For as soon as I heard the sound of your greeting, the child in my womb leaped for joy. And blessed is she who believed that there would be a fulfillment of what was spoken to her by the Lord."*
>
> (Luke 1:39-45) NRSV

Mary stayed with Elizabeth for about three months and then went back home. Finally, six months later her own son was born.

Her Child Is Born

> *In those days a decree went out from Emperor Augustus that all the world should be registered. This was the first registration and was taken*

Bartolomeo Murillo. *The Holy Family at Nazareth,* (1618-1682)

while Quirinius was governor of Syria. All went to their own towns to be registered. Joseph also went from the town of Nazareth in Galilee to Judea, to the city of David called Bethlehem, because he was descended from the house and family of David. He went to be registered with Mary, to whom he was engaged and who was expecting a child. While they were there, the time came for her to deliver her child. And she gave birth to her firstborn son and wrapped him in bands of cloth, and laid him in a manger, because there was no place for them in the inn. In that region there were shepherds living in the fields, keeping watch over their flock by night. Then an angel of the Lord stood before them, and the glory of the Lord shone around them, and they were terrified. But the angel said to them, "Do not be afraid; for see - I am bringing you good news of great joy for all the people: to you is born this day in the city of David a Savior, who is the Messiah, the Lord. This will be a sign for you: you will find a child wrapped in bands of cloth and lying in a manger." And suddenly there was with the angel a multitude of the heavenly host, praising God and saying, "Glory to God in the highest heaven, and on earth peace among those whom he favors! "When the angels had left them and gone into heaven, the shepherds said to one

Filippino Lippi. *The Virgin in Adoration* (Detail), (c. 1457-1504)

another, "Let us go now to Bethlehem and see this thing that has taken place, which the Lord has made known to us." So they went with haste and found Mary and Joseph, and the child lying in the manger. When they saw this, they made known what had been told them about this child; and all who heard it were amazed at what the shepherds told them. But Mary treasured all these words and pondered them in her heart. The shepherds returned, glorifying and praising God for all they had heard and seen, as it had been told them.

(Luke 2:1-20) NRSV

Prophecies in the Temple

After the birth of Jesus, according to St. Luke's Gospel, Mary and Joseph fulfilled what Jewish law customarily required when a child was born. Eight days later, they had the child circumcised and gave him the name Jesus.

After forty days, they took him to the Temple at Jerusalem to consecrate him to God. There, the old man Simeon and the old woman Anna recognized the child's extraordinary mission.

Taking him into his arms, Simeon said to Mary the mother: "You see this child: he is destined

Hector Garrido. *The Shepherds Adore* (Contemporary)

for the fall and for the rising of many in Israel, destined to be a sign that is rejected, and a sword shall pierce your own soul, too, so that the secrets of many hearts may be laid bare."

Then they returned to Galilee, to their own town of Nazareth.

Visit of the Magi

St. Matthew, however, describes less tranquil circumstances following the birth of Christ. When Jesus was born in Bethlehem, Magi from the east arrived to pay him homage, guided by a star. Seeking information of the child's whereabouts from King Herod, they found Jesus with Mary his mother. They offered gifts of gold, frankincense and myrrh. They warned of Herod's purpose to kill the child and departed quickly for their own country by another route.

The Escape to Egypt

"Rise, take the child and his mother," the angel said to Joseph. "Flee to Egypt and stay there till I tell you."

Safe in Mary's arms, Jesus was taken into Egypt where he escaped Herod's massacre of the

Bartolomeo Murillo. *The Holy Family,* (1618-1682)

innocent children of Bethlehem. When, at the angel's command, the child returned to his own land, he had relived the ancient journey of Israel, the Exodus.

Both Matthew and Luke suddenly end their accounts of Jesus' early days when he settled with his family at Nazareth. Except for St. Luke's story of the pilgrimage of the boy Jesus to Jerusalem, the gospels are silent about Jesus and Mary until his public life begins.

Jesus Missing for Three Days

St. Luke relates the story of one pilgrimage the holy family took to Jerusalem:

Every year his parents used to go to Jerusalem for the feast of Passover. When he was twelve years old, they went for the feast as usual.

When they were on their way home after the feast, the boy Jesus stayed behind in Jerusalem without his parents' knowledge. They assumed he was with the caravan, and it was only after a day's journey that they went to look for him among their relations and acquaintances. When they failed to find him, they went back to Jerusalem, looking for him everywhere.

Three days later, they found him in the

Temple, sitting among the doctors, listening to them and asking questions; and all those who heard him were astounded at his intelligence and his answers.

They were overcome when they saw him, and his mother said to him, "My child, why have you done this to us? See how worried your father and I have been, looking for you."

"Why were you looking for me?" he replied. "Did you not know that I must be busy with my Father's affairs?" But they did not understand what he meant.

He then went down with them and came to Nazareth and lived under their authority. His mother stored up all these things in her heart, and Jesus increased in wisdom and stature and grew in favor with God and men.

The Silent Years

His long years at Nazareth are called his "hidden life," the years he grew in "wisdom and age and grace," the years with Mary and Joseph. Nazareth was his first and only school; Mary and Joseph his principal teachers. From them, the Son of God learned to speak his first words, in the accent of Galilee. They acquainted him with the ways of the village and the ways of the human heart. Before anyone else, he listened to and learned from Joseph and Mary.

They taught him to appreciate familiar things from the Galilean hills; the sower, the shepherd and his sheep, the vineyard, the fig tree. These are the images he later used to convey his deepest thoughts.

Ordinary experiences, like watching Mary place a small measure of yeast into flour and seeing it rise before baking gave him early images to describe the remarkable ways the kingdom of God touches all things.

He learned the skills of carpentry and the discipline of hard work at Joseph's side. Joseph, Mary and Jesus seldom went beyond their village and the neighboring fields. Their home was one simple room, used for work by day and as a bedroom by night. There were openings in the limestone floor which fed into grain silos that were carved for storage out of the rock below; on the wall, a niche for an oil lamp, the only light in the windowless room. On summer days, a shelter of branches shaded the flat roof above.

Hector Garrido. *The Sermon on the Mount* (Contemporary)

Though Jerusalem was the center of Jewish worship, the Jewish people of Galilee made the eighty mile journey to the Temple only for the great pilgrimage feasts of Passover, Pentecost and Tabernacles. Their faith was nourished in their home and in the local synagogue. There at Nazareth, Jesus grew to know his own Jewish traditions.

After the Death of Joseph

Joseph's death, some years before Jesus' public ministry, left Mary a widow, depending more than ever on her Son for support.

Devoted to him, she knew he had a mysterious, divine role. Yet, in those long years at Nazareth, she had no heavenly signs to go by. No angel spoke to her; no witnesses came forward to explain anything more of her child's destiny.

At Nazareth Jesus was her faithful Son, working at his trade, following the seasons and the harvests, hardly noticed by his neighbors and relatives. Mary was his mother.

Mary's Imprint on Jesus

It would be natural that Mary's imprint

appear in Jesus' later teachings. The way he valued childhood and family life surely came from rich memories of home life at Nazareth and its simplicity, trust and love.

His later parables and teachings show his esteem for the faith and patience of women and condemn the injustices done to them in the male-dominated society of his time. His advocacy and appreciation for women surely followed his love and respect for the woman who was his mother. He was sensitive to the plight of widows. Surely he was influenced by Mary's situation after the death of Joseph.

Was Jesus' love for his own religious tradition and his ability to be critical of that tradition fostered by the honest sense and devotion of a woman like Mary and a man like Joseph? One thing is certain: Nazareth left an imprint on his experience.

Her Son Leaves Home

When he was about thirty, Jesus left Nazareth to stay for a while in the desert of Judea near the River Jordan where John the Baptist was preaching and baptizing. People said that a prophet had arisen in Israel and that God was speaking in that lonely place.

As she watched her Son go, Mary sensed that the long years of silence were coming to an end.

In those days Jesus came from Nazareth of Galilee and was baptized by John in the Jordan...Now after John was arrested, Jesus came to Galilee, proclaiming the good news of God, and saying, "The time has come near; repent, and believe in the good news."

(Mark 1:9, 14-15) NRSV

He preached in the synagogues around Capernaum on the Lake of Galilee, healing the sick and driving out evil spirits from those who were afflicted. Great crowds flocked to him.

But when he went up to Nazareth, he was rejected.

"Where did this man get all this?" they said when he spoke in their synagogue. "Is he not the carpenter, the son of Mary...?"

"A prophet is not without honor except in his native place and among his own relations and in his own house," Jesus replied, amazed at their lack of faith. He left Nazareth and never returned.

Sees Her Son Rejected

His rejection by his own people undoubtedly caused Mary deep sorrow. She sided with her Son when even some of his own relations thought he had gone mad and wanted to seize him. The old man Simeon had predicted in the Temple when Mary had presented her infant that he would be rejected by his own people.

We don't know where Mary lived during the time of Jesus' public ministry. At Nazareth with some relatives? Or did she move to Capernaum to live among his disciples? Wherever she was, she did not have Jesus as close to her as before.

Jesus' eyes now turned to a larger family.

And he replied, "Who are my mother and my brothers?" And looking at those around him, he said, "Here are my mother and my brothers! Whoever does the will of God is my brother and sister and mother."

(Mark 3:33-35) NRSV

Quietly Following Her Son

Mary had no prominent place in the ministry of Jesus. She was rarely with him.

True, according to John's Gospel, she prompted his first miracle at a wedding feast in Cana of Galilee when he turned water into wine. "Do whatever he tells you," she said to the stewards at the banquet.

Mary mostly remained at a distance while others told her what he said and did. If she had a role during his ministry, it was that of a believer, treasuring in her heart what she heard and trying to understand the meaning of it all. Later, a more active part would be hers.

She followed her Son from afar as he traveled through Galilee to Jerusalem.

"Blessed is the womb that bore you and the breasts that nursed you," some shouted as he passed. And Mary rejoiced at their praise. But she also knew he had powerful enemies whose threats and plots to destroy him increased every day.

When Jesus and his disciples went up to Jerusalem to celebrate the Passover, Mary followed him too, with some relatives and friends. She knew danger awaited them there.

With Her Son as He Dies

> *And this is what the soldiers did. Meanwhile, standing near the cross of Jesus were his mother, and his mother's sister, Mary the wife of Clopas, and Mary Magdalene.*
>
> *(John 19:25) NRSV*

We can hardly guess how Mary experienced the tragic days when they arrested and crucified her Son.

Tradition says she stood on the road as Jesus passed by carrying his cross. When all his disciples fled, she remained with him. Helpless to do anything else, she watched her dying Son and offered her love.

When he died, they took him down from the cross and placed him in her arms. She held him gently, her child of long ago.

Her Joy

She was one of those who saw him risen from the dead. Her cries of grief turned into cries of joy as she waited in prayer with the apostles for the Holy Spirit that Jesus promised to send them.

As the mother of Jesus, Mary had a special place among his followers, strengthening their faith through her own. From his cross, Jesus gave her to his church as a mother for all ages.

We do not know for sure the place or circumstances of Mary's death. One strong tradition attests that she died in Jerusalem. Another tradition points to the city of Ephesus, where she is said to have lived for a while with the apostle John.

Caravaggio. *The Burial of Jesus,* (1571-1610)

MARY IN CHRISTIAN TRADITION

The Scriptures: First Century

> *But when the fullness of time had come, God sent his Son, born of a woman, born under the law.*
> *(Galatians 4:4) NRSV*

Except for this reference, Mary is not mentioned in the earliest Christian writings, the letters of St. Paul. Only the four gospels, written between 65 and 100 A.D., speak of her at any length.

Mark and Luke

Mark's Gospel carries only a brief reference to Mary. It says simply that Jesus is "the son of Mary," omitting any details of his birth or family life. For Mark, belief in Jesus is more important than to have ties of flesh and blood with him. This gospel praises Mary as a believer who does the will of God (Mk 3:31-35) and is a true disciple of her Son.

In Luke's beautiful, extended narration of the events surrounding the birth of Christ, Mary

Sandro Boticelli. *Madonna and Child (Detail)*, (1445-1510)

appears as "the handmaid of the Lord." Drawing, probably, on the devotion of early Jewish-Christians who saw the mother of Jesus as a faithful Israelite living the ordinary life of "the people of the land, "Luke portrays her as a woman of grace, responding to God's mysterious overtures with firm trust and acceptance. Though she questions and does not all together understand God's plan presented by the angel, she believes.

"Be it done to me according to your word", Mary's response to the angel's invitation, is the response every Christian must make in order to transform the events of life and receive God's blessing.

> *And Mary said, "My soul magnifies the Lord, and my spirit rejoices in God my Savior, for he has looked with favor on the lowliness of his servant. Surely, from now on all generations will call me blessed."*
>
> *(Luke 1:46-48) NRSV*

Matthew and John

Matthew's Gospel, intent on tracing Jesus' descent as the Messiah from David through Joseph, presents Mary less prominently than Luke.

Matthew, however, strongly insists on Mary's unique virginal conception: "...before they lived together she was with child through the Holy Spirit" (Mt 1:18). Later, this belief in her virginal conception would bring Mary an honored title, the Mother of God.

John's Gospel, the last of the four, speaks twice of Mary. At Cana in Galilee she intercedes with her Son for a newly married couple and he changes water into wine (Jn 2:1-12). On Calvary she stands beneath the cross at Jesus' death (Jn 19:25-27). The stories of Cana and Calvary led generations of Christians to go to Mary in their need and to rely on her compassion in their suffering.

At Cana and on Calvary Jesus calls his mother "Woman," which early Christian tradition saw as an allusion likening Mary to the first woman, Eve. In God's plan, Mary's faithful response to the angel reversed the failure of Eve and she became the new "mother of all the living."

Later Christian devotion to Mary was nourished primarily by what the four gospels said of her. But other factors, too, contributed to the development of Christian feeling and piety toward the mother of Jesus.

SANTEC VC̄ EPVER PVER HĀ Đ MITE DEO Q ENO PROVND ERTALE RERIP

MARY IN EARLY POPULAR CHRISTIAN LITERATURE

Popular Christian stories about Christ, Mary and the apostles, originating in Syria, Palestine and Egypt from the mid-second century, greatly influenced the way ordinary Christians imagined Mary's life. These stories, attempting to supply details omitted in the gospels, went beyond and sometimes contrary to the indications of the scriptures.

The "Gospel of James," one of these stories written about 150 A.D., portrays the childhood of Mary in this way:

When Mary was one year old, Joachim made a great feast and invited the priest and scribes, and the whole people of Israel assembled. And Joachim brought the child to the priests, and they blessed her saying: O, God of our fathers, bless this child and give her a name renowned for ever among all generations. And all the people said: "So be it, so be it. Amen..."And the child became three years old, and Joachim said: "Call the virgin daughters of the Hebrews and let them accompany the child to the Temple of the Lord with lamps burning in

Pinturicchio. *Madonna and Child Enthroned with Saint John the Baptist* (c. 1454-1513)

their hands." And they went up to the temple of the Lord. And the priests received her and kissed her and blessed her, saying: "The Lord has magnified your name among all generations; in you the Lord will show redemption to the children of Israel." And he sat her on the third step of the altar. And the Lord gave her grace and she danced with her feet and all the house of the Lord loved her. And her parents returned home marveling and praising the Lord because their child did not turn back. And Mary was in the temple of the Lord to be nurtured like a dove; and she received food from the hand of an angel.

By presenting Mary as a sheltered virgin absorbed in serving God in the Temple from her youth, the story sought to defend Christian belief in the virgin birth. Mary lived a protected life before her marriage to Joseph. Yet, unfortunately, the story removed Mary from the ordinary, uneventful village life that scripture suggests was hers.

The account offers details of Mary's marriage to Joseph, who is portrayed as an old widower with his own children, and relates further wonders that accompanied the birth of Jesus in a cave. This early story, which powerfully affected the imagination of Christians, has left its mark on Christian art, liturgy and devotion.

Early Churches and Feasts of Mary

Prompted by this story, in the fifth century a church was built in Jerusalem close by the Temple site honoring Mary's birthplace and home. The ancient church of St. Ann, the mother of Mary, stands on that place today.

The Feasts of the Immaculate Conception (Dec. 8), the Birth of Mary (Sept. 8) and the Presentation of Mary in the Temple (Nov. 21), which are celebrated by many of the Christian churches of the East and West, were also influenced by this popular story.

Mary's Death and Assumption into Heaven

Stories from the fifth century (or perhaps earlier) recount Mary's later life, her death and assumption into heaven, events unreported by the four gospels.

The legends describe Jesus appearing to Mary in the house on Mount Sion in Jerusalem where she lived after Pentecost. Her Son tells her she is soon to die. Then from all parts of the world the apostles gather to bid her farewell:

Stretching out his hands the Lord received her holy soul. And when her soul departed, the place was filled with a sweet smell and bright light. And a voice from heaven proclaimed: "Blessed are you among women." Peter and John, Paul and Thomas, ran to embrace her feet and receive her holiness; and the twelve apostles took her body on a bier and bore it forth. Instructed by Jesus, Peter and the other apostles took her body to be buried in a new tomb near Gethsemane in the Kidron Valley, where miracles of healing accompanied her burial. Three days later, angels took her body to heaven. (Ps John: The Dormition of Mary, 4th century)

By the year 600, a feast called the Dormition of Mary, honoring her death and assumption into heaven, was celebrated in Jerusalem and in the churches of the East. Some centuries later it would pass into the Western churches, known as the Feast of the Assumption of Mary.

Early Palestinian Shrines Honoring Mary

Besides these early stories, devotion to Mary

was nourished by the honor paid to certain ancient sites in Palestine associated with Jesus and his mother:

• At Bethlehem, the grotto of Christ's birth was held sacred.

• At the Mount of Olives outside Jerusalem, grottoes recalling his agony in the garden and ascension were frequented by early Jewish Christians. Mary's grave, too, was honored in this area.

• At Jerusalem, the sites where Jesus died and was buried were remembered.

• On Mount Sion in Jerusalem, the early church met for worship on the site where the Holy Spirit came upon Mary and the disciples at Pentecost.

• At Nazareth, the sites of Jesus' early life were remembered.

Even when Roman armies laid waste to much of Palestine in 70 A.D. and again after the Jewish revolts of 132-135 A.D., Palestinian Christians kept alive the memories and traditions of these holy places where Mary was honored along with her Son.

The Christian "Holy Land" of the Fourth Century

After the Emperor Constantine accepted

Christianity in 313 A.D., he set about making Palestine a vital Christian center of the Roman empire. Under his direction, great churches and shrines were built on the ancient sites of the holy places and Palestine became a land of Christian pilgrimage, a visual gospel.

From 335 A.D. onward, Christian pilgrims from all over the empire, bishops, priests and lay people, flocked to the Holy Land. They wanted to see the manger, the wood of the cross, anything that survived from Jesus' time. Praying at the sacred sites and other shrines, their faith was strengthened. Relics (sometimes authentic, sometimes not) were offered for their devotion. Returning home with their memories and with relics and souvenirs, they celebrated the feasts and sacred places they experienced in the Holy Land in their own liturgies, churches and shrines.

Mary, the mother of Jesus, had a special role in their experience. Her presence in the Holy Land seemed to be everywhere. Devotion to her was nourished by the experience of pilgrimage.

Medieval Devotion to Mary

The Christian people of the Middle Ages

suffered constantly from disease, famine and wars which they were helpless to do anything about. They turned anxiously to Mary for assistance. Their faith led them to trust her to intercede for them with her Son as she did for the ordinary people at the marriage feast of Cana.

Since she was a compassionate mother who experienced the sufferings of Calvary, they petitioned her for cures from sickness, for protection and help. Her kindness and power were proclaimed everywhere; in the sermons they heard, in art and song and prayer.

Meditating on the Life of Mary

Popular classics like *The Meditations on the Life of Christ*, a book dating from the thirteenth century, nourished medieval devotion to Mary.

Widely circulated, it taught Christians to see the lives of Jesus and Mary through a "pilgrimage of the imagination." By meditating on the stories of the gospel, embellished with additional details and legends, one could enter into the world of Christ and his saints and learn from them how to live.

Stories from the *Meditations*, appealing and tender as the following short excerpt from "The

Nativity of Jesus" shows, greatly influenced the way medieval Christians saw Mary and also inspired the works of so many medieval artists.

...the emperor wrote a proclamation that the whole world should be registered, and everyone go to his own city. So obeying the command, Joseph started on his way with our Lady, taking with him an ox and an ass, since she was pregnant and the road was five miles long from Bethlehem to Jerusalem. They arrived like poor owners of animals. Now they could not find an inn when they arrived at Bethlehem, because they were poor and many others were there to register, too. Pity our Lady, and see this delicate girl, only 15 years old, as she walks so carefully, tired by the journey and jostled by the crowds. They were sent away by everyone, the childlike mother and the old man, Joseph, her husband. When they saw an empty cave that people used when it rained, they entered it for shelter. And Joseph, who was an expert carpenter, probably closed it in some way...When Jesus was born Mary wrapped him in the veil from her head and laid him in a manger. The ox and the ass knelt with their mouths above the manger and breathed on the infant as if they knew the child was poorly clothed and needed to be warmed in that cold season. The mother also knelt to adore him and to

Hector Garrido. *Madonna and Child, (Contemporary)*

thank God, saying: "I thank you, Father, that you gave me your Son and I adore you, eternal God, my son." Joseph also adored him. Then Joseph took the ass's saddle and pulled out the stuffing of straw and placed it near the manger so our Lady might rest on it. She sat down and stayed there, her face turned constantly toward the manger, her eyes fixed lovingly on her dear Son.

Mary, the Mother of God: 431 A.D.

Religious controversy also stimulated devotion to Mary in the early church. In 431, the Council of Ephesus repudiated Nestorius, the patriarch of Constantinople, for refusing to honor Mary with the title "Mother of God." Orthodox believers held to the title because it safeguarded Christian belief in the mystery of the Incarnation: Jesus is God and man.

The church did not seek to make Mary a goddess, otherwise she could not have given birth to Christ as someone truly human. She could be called Mother of God, however, because Jesus who was born from her truly was Son of God for all eternity.

Popular feeling for Mary ran high in the Christian world after the Council, and churches

Hector Garrido. *Madonna of the Rock, (Contemporary)*

dedicated to her arose in almost every important city. In the city of Constantinople, an important center of devotion to Mary, 250 churches and shrines in her honor were built before the eighth century. Pictures and icons of Mary holding her divine Child multiplied, especially in the churches of the East, where they became objects of special devotion.

Europe as a Holy Land: 11th - 15th Centuries

The Muslim conquest of Palestine in the seventh century brought the holy places under non-Christian rule that became increasingly hostile toward Christian pilgrims. When the Turks threatened the ancient Christian shrines with destruction, the Christian nations of Europe sought to reconquer the Holy Land in the Crusades of the eleventh century.

During these disturbed times, when pilgrimage was drastically curtailed, the shrines and relics of Palestine were duplicated or transferred to the countries of Europe. In Spain, France, England, Italy, Germany and the Lowlands, great medieval shrines like those in the Holy Land arose in place like Chartres, Monserrat, Walsinham and Loretto. This "European Holy Land" became the setting for the early medieval Christian's devotion to the Mother of God.

In a way similar to this, Christian visionaries, mystics and writers recounted their experience of the gospel stories. The "revelations" of St. Bridgit of Sweden (1303-1373), as well as many popular stories of the gospel, are examples of this meditative approach to the scripture. They influenced Christian devotion to Mary.

The Protestant Reformation

The Protestant reformers of the sixteenth century attacked the low standards that began to harm European devotion to Mary in late medieval times. They condemned superstitious practices exaggerating Mary's power and position, some of which seemed to place her above Christ himself.

Yet Luther or Calvin never rejected veneration of Mary totally. They saw her as a model whose humble faith Christians could imitate. The reformers, however, discouraged Marian pilgrimages and shrines, suppressed her feasts and forbade prayers for her intercession.

The Catholic Church, while acknowledging

abuses to Mary, upheld the privileges and practices which longstanding Christian tradition accorded her as the Mother of Jesus.

Catholic Devotion to Mary from the Reformation to Today

Within the Catholic world of Europe and America, devotion to Mary flourished from the seventeenth century until the time of the Second Vatican Council in the twentieth century. Devotion to Mary during this time strongly influenced every aspect of Roman Catholic culture and piety. Among Eastern and Orthodox Christians also, devotion to Mary continued to be strong.

In the Western church, numerous religious communities and societies, such as the Oblates of Mary Immaculate, the Marists, the Sisters of Notre Dame and the Legion of Mary, were founded under her patronage. They sought to imitate Mary's motherly concern to bring the message of her Son to all peoples through their work in schools, hospitals and missions throughout the world.

The Second Vatican Council

The Second Vatican Council, in its Constitution on the Church (Lumen Gentium), summed up the church's belief about Mary and devotion to her:

We turn our eyes to Mary, a model for all believers. Faithfully meditating on her and contemplating her in light of the Word made man, the church enters more intimately into the great mystery of the Incarnation. For Mary unites in herself the great teachings of faith, and so she calls believers to her Son and his sacrifice and to the love of the Father. Seeking the glory of Christ, the church becomes more like her and progresses in faith, seeking and doing the will of God in all things. Just as the Mother of Jesus, glorified in body and soul in heaven, is the image and beginning of the church as it is to be perfected in the world to come, so, too, does she shine forth on earth, until the day the Lord comes, as a sign of sure solace to the People of God during its sojourn on earth.

(Lumen Gentium 65, 68)

THE ROSARY OF THE BLESSED VIRGIN MARY

The devotion of the Rosary contributes greatly to the destruction of sin, the recovery of grace, and the promotion of the glory of God.
GREGORY XVI

The Rosary is the most popular of all the Marian devotions. It was revealed to St. Dominic by the Blessed Mother, and begun in the fifteenth century by Alen de Rupe, a Dominican preacher. The Rosary combines both vocal and meditative prayer, and is treasured by all who use it. The beginnings of the Rosary are found in the early Christian practice of reciting the 150 Psalms from the Bible, either daily or weekly, as a way of prayer. Those unable to recite the Psalms began to recite 150 prayers, mainly the Our Father, 150 times, often using beads to count the prayers. By medieval times the custom of saying "Paternoster" beads (the latin for Our Father) was common in many countries of Europe. While saying the prayers it was customary to

Bartolomeo Murillo. *Our Lady of the Rosary,* (1618-1682)

meditate on the mysteries of the life of Jesus, from his birth to his resurrection. The Rosary in its present form arose in late medieval Christianity.

The Hail Mary

The Hail Mary evolved as a prayer from the devotion of medieval men and women who saw Mary, the mother of Jesus, as the great witness to his life, death and resurrection. Its earliest form was the greeting made to Mary by the Angel Gabriel:

> *Hail Mary,*
> *full of grace,*
> *the Lord is with you.*   *LUKE 1:28*

Over time the greeting given to Mary by her cousin Elizabeth was added:

> *Blessed are you among women*
> *and blessed is the fruit of your womb.*   *LUKE 1:42*

Finally by the fifteenth century, the remainder of the prayer appeared:

Holy Mary, Mother of God,
pray for us sinners
now and at the hour of our death.

The prayer calls upon Mary, full of grace and close to her Son, to intercede for us sinners now and at the time our death. We share her as a mother with St. John to whom Jesus entrusted her, when on Calvary Jesus said, "Behold your mother." She will always bring Christ into our life. We trust her to care for us as she cared for the newly married couple at Cana in Galilee. We can go to her in our need. By the end of the sixteenth century the practice of saying 150 Hail Marys in series or decades of 10 was popular among many ordinary Christian people. The mysteries of the life, death and resurrection of Jesus, contained in the Joyful, Sorrowful and Glorious Mysteries, were remembered during these prayers.

Rosa Mystica

The name "rosary" comes from the flower, the rose, which in medieval times was seen as a symbol of life eternal. Mary, the first

to be redeemed by Christ, has been called Mystical Rose. She reminds us we are called to the eternal life of Paradise.

How to Say the Rosary

The complete Rosary consists of fifteen decades, but is further divided into three distinct parts, each containing five decades; called the Joyful, the Sorrowful and the Glorious Mysteries. The Mysteries of the Rosary symbolize important events from the lives of both our Lord and the Blessed Mother.

Each decade contains one mystery, an "Our Father," ten "Hail Marys," and a "Glory be to the Father." To say the Rosary, begin by making the sign of the cross and saying "The Apostles' Creed" on the crucifix, one "Our Father" on the first bead, three "Hail Marys" on the next three beads, and then a "Glory be to the Father." When this is finished, meditate upon the first mystery, say an "Our Father," ten "Hail Marys," and one "Glory be to the Father." The first decade is now completed, and to finish the Rosary proceed in the same manner until all five decades have been said.

Hector Garrido. *Our Lady of Grace,* (Contemporary)

The Five Joyful Mysteries

Mondays and Thursdays

1. **The Annunciation**
   The Angel Gabriel tells Mary that she is
   to be the Mother of God.   *Humility*

2. **The Visitation**
   The Blessed Virgin pays a visit to her
   cousin Elizabeth.   *Charity*

3. **The Nativity**
   The Infant Jesus is born in a stable at
   Bethlehem.   *Poverty*

4. **The Presentation**
   The Blessed Virgin presents the Child
   Jesus to Simeon in the Temple. *Obedience*

5. **The Finding in the Temple**
   Jesus is lost for three days, and the
   Blessed Mother finds him in the Temple.
   Piety

The Five Sorrowful Mysteries

Tuesdays and Fridays

1. **The Agony in the Garden**
   Jesus prays in the Garden of Olives and drops of blood break through his skin.
   Contrition

2. **The Scourging at the Pillar**
   Jesus is tied to a pillar and cruelly beaten with whips. *Purity*

3. **The Crowning with Thorns**
   A crown of thorns is placed upon Jesus' head. *Courage*

4. **The Carrying of the Cross**
   Jesus is made to carry his cross to Calvary. *Patience*

5. **The Crucifixion**
   Jesus is nailed to the cross, and dies for our sins. *Self-denial*

The Five Glorious Mysteries

Wednesdays, Saturdays and Sundays

1. **The Resurrection**
   Jesus rises from the dead, three days
   after his death.   *Faith*

2. **The Ascension**
   Forty days after his death, Jesus ascends
   into heaven.   *Hope*

3. **The Descent of the Holy Spirit**
   Ten days after the Ascension, the Holy
   Spirit comes to the apostles and the
   Blessed Mother in the form of fiery
   tongues.   *Love*

4. **The Assumption**
   The Blessed Virgin dies and is
   assumed into heaven.   *Eternal Happiness*

5. **The Crowning of the Blessed Virgin**
   The Blessed Virgin is crowned Queen of
   Heaven and Earth by Jesus, her Son.
                                Devotion to Mary

Hail, Holy Queen

Hail, holy Queen, Mother of mercy, our life, our sweetness, and our hope.

To you we cry, poor banished children of Eve; to you we send up our sighs, mourning and weeping in this valley of tears.

Turn then, O most gracious advocate, your eyes of mercy toward us, and after this our exile, show unto us the blessed fruit of your womb, Jesus.

O clement, O loving, O sweet Virgin Mary.

V. Pray for us, O holy Mother of God,

R. That we may be made worthy of the promises of Christ.

Let us pray.

O God, whose only begotten Son, by his life, death and resurrection, has purchased for us the rewards of eternal life, grant, we beseech you, that meditating upon these Mysteries of the most Holy Rosary of the Blessed Virgin Mary, we may imitate what they contain and obtain what they promise.

Through the same Christ our Lord. Amen.

APPARITIONS OF MARY

In recent centuries, apparitions of Mary reported at Lourdes (1858) in France, Knock (1879) in Ireland, Fatima (1917) in Portugal and other places created widespread interest among Catholics throughout the world. Mary, appearing to people who were mostly uneducated, often only children, called for worldwide repentance and a renewal of faith in her Son.

Many ordinary people suffering from poverty created by the Industrial Revolution and the destructiveness of modern warfare saw these apparitions of Mary as a sign from heaven that God still cared for his people.

Miracles of healing were reported at these shrines, which became new popular centers of devotion to the Mother of God.

Traditional Marian shrines such as Guadalupe in Mexico and Our Lady of Czestochowa in Poland continued to be rallying places and centers of spiritual, cultural and political influence in the nations and among their people.

Our Lady of the Miraculous Medal

This devotion was begun by Catherine Laboure, a French Sister of the Daughters of Charity. She was born on a farm in France in 1806.

In 1830, Catherine experienced three apparitions of Mary. In one apparition, Catherine saw a picture of Mary standing on a globe with light streaming from her hands. Around the Virgin were the words: "O Mary conceived without sin, pray for us who have recourse to you." Mary entrusted this devotion to Catherine, and told her to have a holy medal made with the picture of Mary, the Immaculate Conception, stamped on it.

As soon as people began wearing the medal, miracles started happening. The medal soon began to be called the "Miraculous Medal."

Catherine never told anyone but her confessor about the visions. So, even at her death in 1876, no one knew that Catherine was the one who brought the Miraculous Medal to the world.

Prayer to Our Lady of the Miraculous Medal

O Virgin Mother of God, Mary Immaculate, we dedicate and consecrate ourselves to you under the title of Our Lady of the Miraculous Medal.

May this medal be for each one of us a sure sign of your affection for us and a constant reminder of our duties toward you.

Ever while wearing it, may we be blessed by your loving protection and preserved in the grace of your Son.

O most powerful Virgin, Mother of our Savior, keep us close to you every moment of our lives.

Obtain for us, your children, the grace of a happy death; so that, in union with you, we may enjoy the bliss of heaven forever. Amen.

O Mary, conceived without sin, pray for us who have recourse to you.

(3 times)

Our Lady of Fatima

One of the most powerful of Mary's apparitions in modern times was to three peasant children near Fatima, Portugal, in May 1917. The three children were Lucia, Francisco and Jacinta Marta. They saw the figure of a lady brighter than the sun, standing on a cloud in an evergreen tree. They were granted six apparitions between May and October 1917. Each took place on the 13th of the month, except in August, when the date was the 19th.

On October 13, when Lucia asked the Lady who she was and what she wanted, she replied with these words: "I am Our Lady of the Rosary; I wish to have a chapel in my honor on this spot. Continue to recite the Rosary every day. People must mend their ways, ask pardon for their sins, and no longer offend our Lord, who is already too much offended."

Her message at Fatima was to accept life's sufferings and continue to pray for the people throughout the world.

Hector Garrido. *Our Lady of Fatima, (Contemporary)*

Prayer to Our Lady of Fatima

Most Holy Virgin, who appeared at Fatima, to reveal to the three little shepherds the treasures of graces hidden in the recitation of the Rosary: Inspire our hearts with a sincere love of this devotion, in order that by meditating on the Mysteries of our Redemption that are recalled in it, we may gather the fruits and obtain the conversion of sinners, and (here name the other favors you are praying for), which we ask of you in this Novena, for the greater glory of God, for your own honor, and for the good of souls. Amen.

Our Lady of the Rosary of Fatima, pray for us.

Our Lady of Lourdes

One celebrated apparition of Our Lady took place at Lourdes in the southwest of France in 1858. From February 11 to July 16, 1858, the Virgin appeared eighteen times in the hollow of a cave, on the edge of a mountain stream, to a little girl named Bernadette Soubirous, who came from a very poor family.

During the ninth apparition, on February 25, the Lady asked Bernadette to drink from a spring. As none was visible, the child scooped away sand at the back of the cave, knelt and drank of the water that welled up. The next day a spring was flowing, which produced an abundant supply of water even till today.

On March 24 the Lady said to Bernadette in the local dialect, "I am the Immaculate Conception," and asked for prayer and penance for the conversion of peoples. Mary's request that a chapel be built at the Grotto and spring was fulfilled in 1862.

Prayer to Our Lady of Lourdes

O Immaculate Virgin, mother of mercy, health of the sick, refuge of sinners, comforter of the afflicted, you know my wants, my troubles, my sufferings; look upon us in mercy.

By appearing in the Grotto of Lourdes to St. Bernadette, you were pleased to make it a privileged sanctuary, whence you dispense your favors, and many have already obtained the cure of their infirmities, both spiritual and corporal. I come, therefore, with the most unbounded confidence to implore your maternal intercession.

Obtain for me, O loving Mother, what I request (here mention your request). Through gratitude for your favors, I will endeavor to imitate your virtues, that I may one day share your glory.

Our Lady of Lourdes, Mother of Christ, you had influence with your divine Son while upon earth. You have the same influence now in heaven.

Pray for me; obtain for me from your divine Son my special request if it be your divine will. Amen.

Feast Day: February 11

Hector Garrido. *Our Lady of Lourdes with Saint Bernadette,* (Contemporary)

Our Lady of Guadalupe

On December 9, 1531, the Blessed Virgin appeared on the Tepeyec hill, then about three miles outside of Mexico City, to Juan Diego, an Indian convert.

She told the poor Indian she wished a shrine built there. When Juan Diego told Bishop Zumarraga of the request, he refused to believe him and asked a sign be given.

Three days later, the Blessed Mother appeared again to Juan and told him to gather roses from the hillside, put them in his poor cloak and give them to the Bishop. Though it was December – not the time for roses at all – Juan gathered the roses and presented them to the bishop.

Impressed on the poor Indian's cloak, the bishop saw a picture of Our Lady of Guadalupe.

Guadalupe is one of the great Marian shrines in the world. Pope Pius XII declared Our Lady of Guadalupe the patroness of the Americas.

Hector Garrido. *Our Lady of Guadalupe, (Contemporary)*

Prayer to Our Lady of Guadalupe

Our Lady of Guadalupe,
mystical rose,
make intercession for Holy Church,
protect the sovereign pontiff,
help all those who invoke you in their
necessities, and since you art the ever Virgin
Mary and
Mother of the true God,
obtain for us from your most holy Son
the grace of keeping our faith,
sweet hope in the midst of the bitterness of life,
burning charity and
the precious gift of final perseverance.

Feast Day: December 12

Our Lady of Vladimir

One of the most famous and most beautiful of all icons of Mary is that of Vladimir. She is depicted cheek to cheek with the Christ Child, whose arms hold her.

It is a good example of the icon the Russians call tenderness. It was probably painted in Constantinople in the twelfth century, but was first noted in Kiev, where it was taken in 1155 to the city of Vladimir.

It became famous for wonders and was worshiped as Russia's most sacred image. In 1395 it was enshrined in the cathedral of the Assumption in the Kremlin in Moscow. Several times the Tartars were beaten back under its inspiration and it was carried to critical places in times of distress; the last time to the battlefront during World War I.

Until the revolution, all the czars were crowned and patriarchs installed in the presence of this image. The Russian calendar commemorates the feast of Our Lady of Vladimir on May 21.

Prayer to Our Lady of Vladimir

O Blessed Lady, with Jesus always before you,
You watch over all your children.
You resist war and persecution,
and so we come before you with confidence
to implore your motherly intercesion.
We beseech you to help end all division,
violence and persecution.
We look for your protection in our trials.
Remove all that separates us from one another,
and lead us into unity with Jesus.
Hear our prayer, O Blessed Lady,
and draw us closer to each other. Amen.

Our Lady of Czestochowa

The icon of Our Lady of Czestochowa, also known as the Black Madonna, is enshrined on the Jasna Gora (hill of light) above the city of Czestochowa in South Central Poland. Here under this title the Polish people for centuries have honored Mary the Mother of God and her divine Son.

In 1382, the painting of the Black Madonna was brought to the shrine atop Jasna Gora in a monastery run by the Pauline Fathers. The painting was defaced with a sword by thieves, and marks can still be seen on Mary's face to this day.

Since 1656, after the great victory of Poland over Sweden, Our Lady of Czestochowa has been worshiped as a Queen of Poland.

The people of Poland have made Czestochowa a center of pilgrimage and the center of their nation. In the years under Communist domination, the shrine of Our Lady of Czestochowa became the rallying point for the Polish people, who were persecuted for their faith.

Our Lady of Czestochowa

Prayer to Our Lady of Czestochowa

(To be said each day upon arising)

Holy Mother of Czestochowa,
you are full of grace, goodness
and mercy. I consecrate to you all my
thoughts, words and actions; especially my
soul and body. I ask for your blessings
and especially prayers for my
salvation. Today, I dedicate myself to you,
good Mother, totally; with my body and
soul, amid joy and suffering,
to obtain for myself and others your
blessings on this earth and eternal life in
heaven. Amen.

Our Lady of Perpetual Help

This title is connected with a Byzantine icon which was stolen from Crete, brought to Rome, and according to tradition (upon the instructions of Our Lady) was placed in the Augustinian Church of St. Matthew in Rome. After the destruction of the church in 1798, the image was given to the Redemptorists who placed it in the church of St. Alfonso, built on the same site.

The inscription in Greek above Our Lady means, "Mother of God"; above the child, "Jesus Christ"; above the angels with the instrument of the Passion of Christ, "Michael" and "Gabriel." Jesus looks with fear at the instruments of his future Passion and clasped with his little hands the hand of his Mother.

Prayer to Our Lady of Perpetual Help

O Mother of Perpetual Help, with greatest
confidence I present myself to you.
I implore your help in the
problems of my daily life.
Trials and sorrows often depress me;
painful privations bring heartache into my
life; often I meet the cross.
Have pity on me, compassionate Mother.
Take care of my needs,
free me from my sufferings or, if it be the will
of God that I should suffer still longer,
grant that I may endure all
with love and patience.
Mother of Perpetual Help,
I ask this in your love and power.

Our Lady of Mount Carmel

In biblical times, Mount Carmel in the Holy Land was honored as a holy place. There the Prophet Elijah, who called kings to account, communed with God, and God strengthened his tired spirit. Once from the mountain, the prophet saw a small cloud coming from the sea, bringing rain to a land dry and without water. His own soul was nourished then as well.

Christian hermits settled on the holy mountain and by the twelfth century were known as "Brothers of Our Lady of Mount Carmel," for they were devoted to Mary, the Mother of Jesus, who meditated on the mysteries of her Son and "treasured all these things in her heart." They sought her intercession; like the cloud she brought life to a parched world: her Son, Jesus Christ.

From Mount Carmel the community spread into Europe where Christians welcomed their devotion to Mary and their contemplative spirituality. They were known as Carmelites.

The feast of Our Lady of Mount Carmel is celebrated on July 16.

Hector Garrido. *Our Lady of Mount Carmel, (Contemporary)*

Prayer to Our Lady of Mount Carmel

Most beautiful flower of Mount Carmel,
fruitful vine, splendor of heaven,
Mother of the Son of God and Immaculate
Virgin, assist me in my hour of need.
Star of the Sea, help me and
show me that you are my mother.
Holy Mary, Mother of God, Queen of heaven
and earth, I humbly ask you from the bottom of
my heart, to assist me in my hour of need. There
are none that can withstand your power.
Show me that you are my mother. Mary,
conceived without sin, pray for us who have
recourse to you.
(3 times)
Dear Mother, I place this cause in your hands.
(3 times)

Feast Day: July 16

Our Lady of Knock

In the early evening of August 21, 1879, a small crowd of people saw three figures hovering against the wall of the local church in the town of Knock, in County Mayo, in the north-west of Ireland. The figures remained there for about a half hour, not speaking a word. The crowd identified them as Mary, St. Joseph and St. John the Baptist.

Large numbers of pilgrims began coming to Knock, and cures of the sick have taken place there over the years. A large basilica of Our Lady of Knock, holding 15,000 people, is the center of devotion to Mary in Ireland and attracts the faithful from other parts of the world as well.

Prayer to
Our Lady of Knock
Eleventh Century Irish Litany of Mary

Great Mary,
Greatest of Marys,
Greatest of Women,
Mother of Eternal Glory,
Mother of the Golden Light,
Honor of the Sky,
Temple of the Divinity,
Fountain of the Gardens,
Serene as the Moon,
Bright as the Sun,
Garden Enclosed,
Temple of the Living God,
Light of Nazareth,
Beauty of the World,
Queen of Life,
Ladder of Heaven,
Mother of God.

Pray for us.

PRAYERS TO THE BLESSED VIRGIN MARY

The Hail Mary

Hail Mary, full of grace,
   the Lord is with you.
   Blessed are you among women,
   and blessed is the fruit
   of your womb, Jesus.

Holy Mary, Mother of God,
   pray for us sinners,
   now and at the hour of our death. Amen.

The Memorare

Remember, O most gracious Virgin Mary,
   that never was it known that
   anyone who fled to your protection,
   implored your help,
   or sought your intercession
   was left unaided.

Inspired by this confidence, we fly unto you,
   O Virgin of virgins, our Mother!

To you we come, before you we stand,
   sinful and sorrowful.

O Mother of the Word incarnate,
   despise not our petitions, but in your
   mercy hear and answer us. Amen.

The Magnificat

My soul proclaims the greatness
    of the Lord and my spirit
    exults in God my savior;
    because he has looked upon his
    lowly handmaid.
Yes, from this day forward
    all generations will call me blessed,
    for the Almighty
    has done great things for me.
Holy is his name, and his mercy reaches
    from age to age
    for those who fear him.
He has shown the power of his arm,
    he has routed the proud of heart.
He has pulled down princes
    from their thrones and
    exalted the lowly.
The hungry he has filled with good
    things, the rich sent empty away.
He has come to the help of Israel
    his servant, mindful of his mercy –
    according to the promise he made
    to our ancestors – of his mercy to
    Abraham and to his descendants
    for ever.

Hector Garrido. *Madonna of the Night,* (Contemporary)

The Regina Caeli
"Queen of Heaven"

Queen of heaven, rejoice, Alleluia.
  The Son whom you were privileged to bear,
   Alleluia, has risen as he said, Alleluia.

Pray to God for us, Alleluia.

Rejoice and be glad, Virgin Mary, Alleluia.
  For the Lord has truly risen. Alleluia.

Let us pray. O God
  it was by the Resurrection of
  your Son,
  our Lord Jesus Christ,
  that you brought joy to the world.

Grant that through the intercession of the Virgin Mary, his Mother, we may attain the joy of eternal life.

Through Christ, our Lord. Amen.

The Angelus

The angel of the Lord declared unto Mary.

And she conceived of the Holy Spirit. Hail
Mary…

Behold the handmaid of the Lord.

Be it done to me according to your word.
Hail Mary…

And the Word was made flesh;
and dwelt among us. Hail Mary…

Pray for us, O holy Mother of God, that we
may be made worthy
of the promises of Christ.

Let us pray.

Pour forth, we beseech you, O Lord, your
grace in our hearts, that we, to whom
the Incarnation of Christ, your Son,
was made known
by the message of an angel,
may by his passion and cross
be brought to the glory of his
resurrection; through the same Christ
our Lord.
Amen.

Litany of the Blessed Virgin Mary

Lord, have mercy,

Christ, have mercy,

Lord, have mercy.

Christ, hear us.

Christ, graciously hear us.

God, the Father of heaven, have mercy on us.

God, the Son, Redeemer of the world, have mercy on us.

God, the Holy Spirit, have mercy on us.

Holy Trinity, one God, have mercy on us.

Holy Mary,

(after each invocation, respond with, "Pray for us")

-Pray for us.

Holy Mother of God,

Holy Virgin of virgins,

Mother of Christ,

Mother, full of grace,

Mother most pure,

Mother most chaste,

Immaculate Mother,

Sinless Mother,

Lovable Mother,

Model of mothers,

Bartolomeo Murillo. *The Immaculate Conception,* (1618-1682)

Mother of good counsel,
Mother of our Maker,
Mother of our Savior,
Wisest of virgins,
Holiest of virgins,
Virgin, powerful in the sight of God,
Virgin, merciful to us sinners,
Virgin, faithful to all God asks of you,
Mirror of holiness,
Seat of wisdom,
Cause of our joy,
Shrine of the Spirit,
Honor of your people,
Devoted handmaid of the Lord,
Mystical Rose,
Tower of David,
Tower of ivory,
House of gold,
Ark of the covenant,
Gate of heaven,
Star of hope,
Health of the sick,
Refuge of sinners,
Comfort of the afflicted,
Help of Christians,

Queen of angels,
Queen of patriarchs,
Queen of prophets,
Queen of apostles,
Queen of martyrs,
Queen of confessors,
Queen of virgins,
Queen of all saints,
Queen conceived in holiness,
Queen raised up to glory,
Queen of the Rosary,
Queen of peace,
Lamb of God, you take away the sins
   of the world, – Spare us, O Lord.
Lamb of God, you take away the sins
   of the world,
          – Graciously hear us, O Lord.
Lamb of God, you take away the sins
   of the world, – Have mercy on us.

Pray for us, O holy Mother of God,
   – That we may be made worthy
         of the promises of Christ.

Let us pray.
Lord God,
   give to your people the joy of

continual health in mind and body.

With the prayers of the Virgin Mary
　　to help us, guide us through
　　the sorrows of this life to
　　eternal happiness in the life to come.

We ask this through Christ our Lord.
　　Amen.

Marian Year Prayer of Pope John Paul II

Mother of the Redeemer,
with great joy we call you blessed.
In order to carry out
his providential plan of salvation,
God the Father chose you
before the creation of the world.
You believed in his love
and obeyed his word.
The Son of God desired you for his Mother
when he became man to save the human race.
You received him
with ready obedience and undivided heart.
as his mystical spouse,
and he filled you with singular gifts.
You allowed yourself to be led
by his hidden and powerful action.

Hector Garrido. *Bethlehem,* (Contemporary)　　　　*103*

FEASTS OF MARY

The Calendar of the Catholic Church, with its feasts, scriptural readings and prayers, is a good guide to Christian belief about Mary and her role in our life. The universal calendar, revised in 1970, celebrates feasts of Mary almost every month. There are major feasts of Mary and feasts of lesser rank. Many of Mary's feasts originate early on in the churches of the East and are still celebrated by them today.

Besides feasts devoted particularly to Mary, she has an important place in feasts of our Lord, like the Feast of Christmas, the Annunciation, the Visitation and the Presentation. They too help us to know her part in the mystery of salvation.

Major Feasts of Mary

The major feasts of Mary offer the most important reasons for honoring her and explain our relationship to her. They contain the substance of the Church's Marian belief. They offer Mary to us as a model for believers, who calls us to imitate her pilgrim faith.

William Bouguereau. *Madonna and Child with Angel Choir,*
(1825-1905)

The Solemnity of Mary, the Mother of God.
(January 1)

This feast, closely connected to the Feast of Christmas, is chief and oldest of the major feasts of Mary. It points to the source of her privileges: her motherhood.

Mary, therefore, is not simply a passive instrument in God's hands; she discovered and accepted new dimensions to her motherhood as her life unfolded.

Along with the Byzantine and Syrian churches, which celebrate the feast of the Mother of God (Theotokos) on December 26, the Roman church celebrates this primary feast close to the Feast of the Birth of Jesus Christ.

The Immaculate Conception of Mary
(December 8)

Like the Solemnity of Mary, the Mother of God, the Feast of the Immaculate Conception, celebrated during Advent, is related to the mystery of Jesus. To fulfill her unique role in the mission of Jesus, Mary was conceived free from original sin through the foreseen merits of her Son.

The Feast of the Conception of Mary

appeared in the Roman calendar in 1476. After the dogmatic definition of 1854, it became the Feast of the Immaculate Conception.

The Assumption of Mary
(August 15)

As the Feast of the Immaculate Conception proclaims the grace of Christ in Mary before he was born, so the Feast of the Assumption points to the fulfillment of that grace, when Mary was taken, body and soul, into heaven to share in the glory of her Son's Resurrection. This feast has its roots in the early Jerusalem church and in the churches of the East.

Feasts of the Lord

The Presentation of the Lord in the Temple
(February 2)

The Feast of the Presentation, an ancient feast also with roots in the early Jerusalem church, celebrates the day when Mary and Joseph brought their infant Child to the Temple of Jerusalem to present him to God according to Jewish custom. Though a feast of Jesus Christ, who is revealed

Hector Garrido. *Madonna and Child,* (Contemporary)

as Messiah to the aged Simeon and Anna, faithful Israelites waiting for the Messiah, it is also is a feast of Mary.

The Annunciation of the Lord
(March 25)

The feast , recalling the angel Gabriel's visit to Nazareth to announce to Mary God's invitation that she should be the mother of a Divine Son, is primarily a feast of Jesus Christ. It celebrates God become incarnate, the Word made flesh, as a loving gift to humanity and all creation. Yet Mary had an important role in the mystery of the Incarnation.

Though troubled by the angel's extraordinary words, Mary accepts the invitation in faith. "Behold the handmaid of the Lord; let it be done to me according to your word". (Lk 1:38)

The feast is celebrated nine months before the feast of Jesus' birth.

The Visitation
(May 31)

The Feast of the Visitation celebrates Mary's visit to her cousin Elizabeth who was with child. At their meeting, John the Baptist, the child in Elizabeth's womb, leapt for joy, and Elizabeth cried out in a loud voice, "Blessed are you among women and blessed is the fruit of your womb". (Lk 1:41). Jesus Christ, in Mary's womb, is recognized as God's blessing.

The Feast of the Visitation is celebrated between the Feast of the Annunciation and the Feast of the Birth of John the Baptist (June 24).

Other Feasts of Mary

The major feasts of Mary and feasts of our Lord in which she has a special place present the essential teaching of the Church about her.

Mary is also honored in other feasts, some ancient and others of more recent origin. The feasts of the Birth of the Blessed Virgin Mary and her Presentation in the Temple arose from stories and celebrations of the early Jerusalem church. Other feasts of Mary, like the feast of Our Lady of Lourdes, celebrate more recent appearances and devotions.

One should remember that the Catholic Church's approval of apparitions, like Lourdes, or of private revelations, like devotion to the Miraculous

Medal, is not an infallible confirmation of their historical truth, but rather an assertion by the Church, after investigation, that this special place or way of venerating Mary can bring spiritual nourishment to those who are drawn to it. They encourage people to prayer, penance and the celebration of sacraments.

The Birth of the Blessed Virgin Mary (September 8)

Three important births are celebrated in the Roman calendar: the birth of Jesus, of Mary and of John the Baptist (June 24). Mary's birth has been celebrated from ancient times, though her birthplace or time of birth are not mentioned in scripture. As far back as the fifth century a church was built on the traditional site of her birth in Jerusalem on the site of the pool of Bethsaida, near the Temple, and a feast in honor of Mary's birth was celebrated. By the eighth century the feast was celebrated in the Church of Rome.

The Presentation of the Blessed Virgin Mary (November 21)

The present memorial of Mary's presentation in the Temple as a child originated in Jerusalem at the church built there in her honor. It celebrates Mary's dedication to God. The feast became popular in the Western church in religious communities, where members renewed their vows on this day, remembering the one who called herself "the maidservant of the Lord."

Dedication of St. Mary Major
(August 5)

This optional memorial celebrates the dedication of the great church of St. Mary Major, built in Rome after the Council of Ephesus in 431. Still one of the main churches of the Eternal City, the church was built to honor Mary as the Mother of God and reflected the growing devotion to her among Christians everywhere. One of the great icons of Mary is revered in this ancient Roman Church.

Our Lady of Mount Carmel
(July 16)

The feast, an optional celebration, was originally celebrated by the Carmelite order in Europe in the Middle Ages. It was first listed in the Roman calendar in 1726.

Our Lady of the Rosary
(October 7)

Originally this feast was celebrated in thanksgiving for Mary's intercession, after the defeat on October 7, 1571, of Turkish naval forces that threatened Europe. Today the feast is a special remembrance of the spiritual power of the Rosary.

Our Lady of Sorrows
(September 15)

Christians of the Middle Ages and later centuries developed a lively devotion to Mary in her sorrows, which were foretold by the old man, Simeon, when she brought the Child Jesus into the Temple. As the first disciple of her Son, she entered into his paschal mystery, and her motherhood matured and took new form as she accepted her part of his cross.

In fact, Mary is a model for Christians who wish to follow the words of Jesus, "Take up your cross each day and follow me." We seek in her faith support for our own.

In the Western church, religious orders, especially the Order of Servites, promoted devotion to the Sorrowful Mother.

Traditionally, seven sorrows are ascribed to her:

1. Mary hears the prophecy of sorrow from Simeon.
2. Mary flees with the Child into Egypt.
3. Mary experiences the loss of the Child Jesus in Jerusalem.
4. Mary meets her Son on the road to Calvary.
5. Mary stands beneath the cross of Jesus.
6. Mary receives the body of Jesus taken down from the cross.
7. Mary sees her Son's body placed in the tomb.

Today the Feast of Our Lady of Sorrows is celebrated the day after the Feast of the Holy Cross.

The Queenship of Mary
(August 22)

In the Old Testament, royal titles are commonly given to God and those specially anointed by God. Titles of royalty were given to Jesus and Mary from earliest times by Christians as signs of the special power they possessed. In

Hector Garrido. *The Assumption of Mary,* (Contemporary)

prayers and hymns like the Salve Regina and the Regina Coeli, Mary, the Mother of Jesus, is called Queen.

Instituted in 1955, this feast follows the Feast of the Assumption, as it points to Mary's privileged place in heaven. Mary "was taken up body and soul into heavenly glory when her earthly life was over, and exalted by the Lord as Queen over all things" (Vatican Council, Lumen Gentium 59).

Our Lady of Guadalupe
(December 12)

Under the title of Our Lady of Guadalupe, Mary is honored as the "patroness of the Americas." The feast originated in the apparition of the Blessed Virgin to Juan Diego, a humble Mexican worker, in 1531.

Our Lady of Lourdes
(February 11)

Pope Pius X included the Feast of Our Lady of Lourdes in the Roman calendar in 1908, just fifty years after the report of Mary's apparitions at the grotto of Massabielle near

Hector Garrido. *Praying Madonna, (Contemporary)*

Lourdes, in France. There Mary identified herself as the Immaculate Conception.

Immaculate Heart of Mary
(Saturday after the Feast of the Sacred Heart)

Closely related to the Feast of the Sacred Heart of Jesus, the optional memorial of the Immaculate Heart of Mary was instituted in 1942. The feast honors Mary who treasured the mysteries of Jesus and "pondered them in her heart."

Other Feasts and Times Dedicated to Mary

Besides the feasts of Mary in the Roman calendar, she is honored in the particular calendars of various rites, nations, regions and religious communities. Since the eighteenth century, the calendar months of May and October have been devoted to Mary in the Roman Catholic Church. Originating in Spain and Italy, where Mary was honored with "May Devotions," litanies, the Rosary and other special prayers, the practice spread worldwide.

Feasts of Mary

January 1: Solemnity of Mary, the Mother of God

February 2: Presentation of Jesus in the Temple

February 11: Our Lady of Lourdes

March 25: The Annunciation

May 31: The Visitation
The Immaculate Heart of Mary

July 16: Our Lady of Mount Carmel

August 5: Dedication of St. Mary Major

August 15: The Assumption of Our Lady

August 22: The Queenship of Mary

September 8: The Birth of Mary

September 15: Our Lady of Sorrows

October 7: Our Lady of the Rosary

November 21: The Presentation of Mary

December 8: The Immaculate Conception

December 12: Our Lady of Guadalupe

December 25: Christmas, the Birth of Our Lord

Bibliography

At Worship with Mary, Christopher O'Donnell, Wilmington, Delaware, 1988

Behold Your Mother: Woman of Faith, National Conference of Catholic Bishops, Washington, 1973

Catechism of the Catholic Faith, New York, 1995

Image and Pilgrimage in Christian Culture, Victor Turner and Edith Turner, New York, 1978

Mary, A History of Doctrine and Devotion, Hilda Graef, Westminster, Maryland, 1965

Roman Calendar, Text and Commentary, U.S. Catholic Conference, Washington, 1976

The Mother of the Redeemer, Pope John Paul II, Washington, 1987

Theotokos, A Theological Encyclopedia of the Blessed Virgin Mary, Michael O'Carroll, C.S.Sp., Wilmington, Delaware, 1982

The Saints of the New Testament, Victor Hoagland, C.P., New York 1999